Esa-Pekka Salonen

LACHEN VERLERNT

for solo violin

CHESTER MUSIC

Lachen verlernt was commissioned by the La Jolla Chamber Music Society's SummerFest La Jolla, with the generous support of Joan & Irwin Jacobs. It was first performed on 10th August 2002 at SummerFest La Jolla, San Diego, California, by Cho-Liang Lin, Artistic Director of the Festival.

Duration: c. 10 minutes
Score available on sale: Order No. CH 65747

Pages 8 and 9 are also included as a separate sheet, to facilitate page turns.

Note: the title *Lachen verlernt* (Laughing unlearnt) is taken from a line in the song, 'Prayer to Pierrot', from Schoenberg's *Pierrot Lunaire*, in which the narrator entreats the harlequin, Pierrot, to teach her to laugh again.

LACHEN VERLERNT
for solo violin

Esa-Pekka Salonen

CH65747

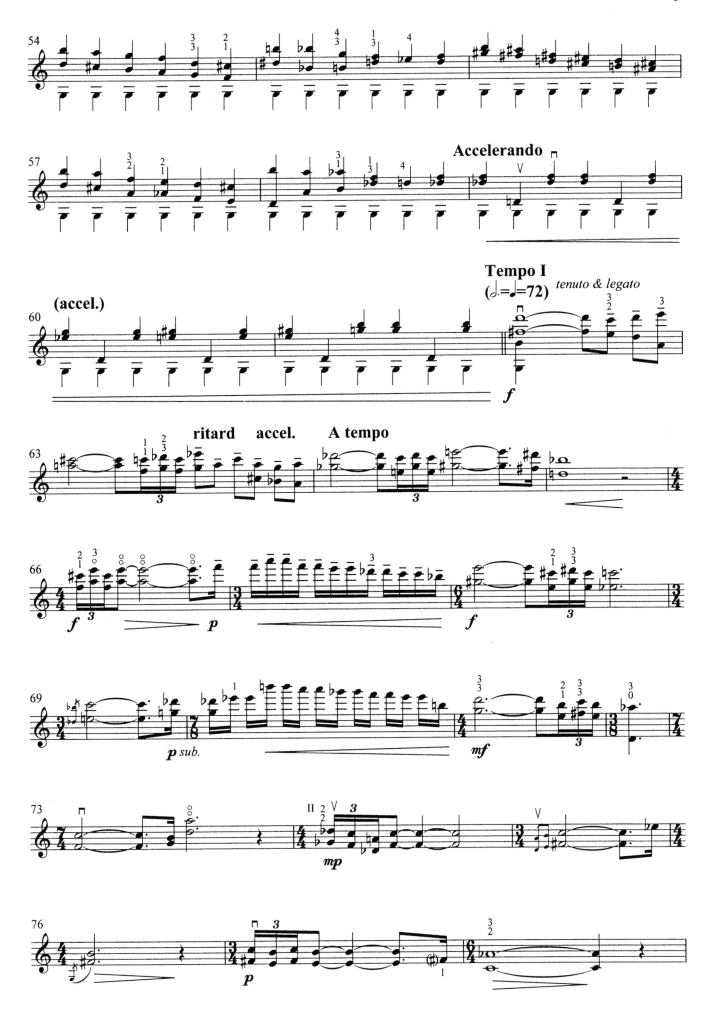

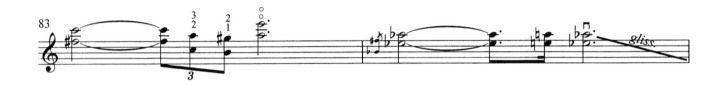

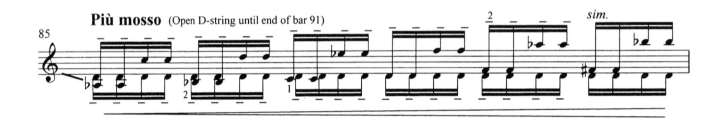

Esa-Pekka Salonen

LACHEN VERLERNT

pages 8 & 9

Lachen verlernt

Lachen verlernt

Rallentando & diminuendo al Fine

Lento assai

dim. al niente

Sipoo, Finland, 11 July 2002

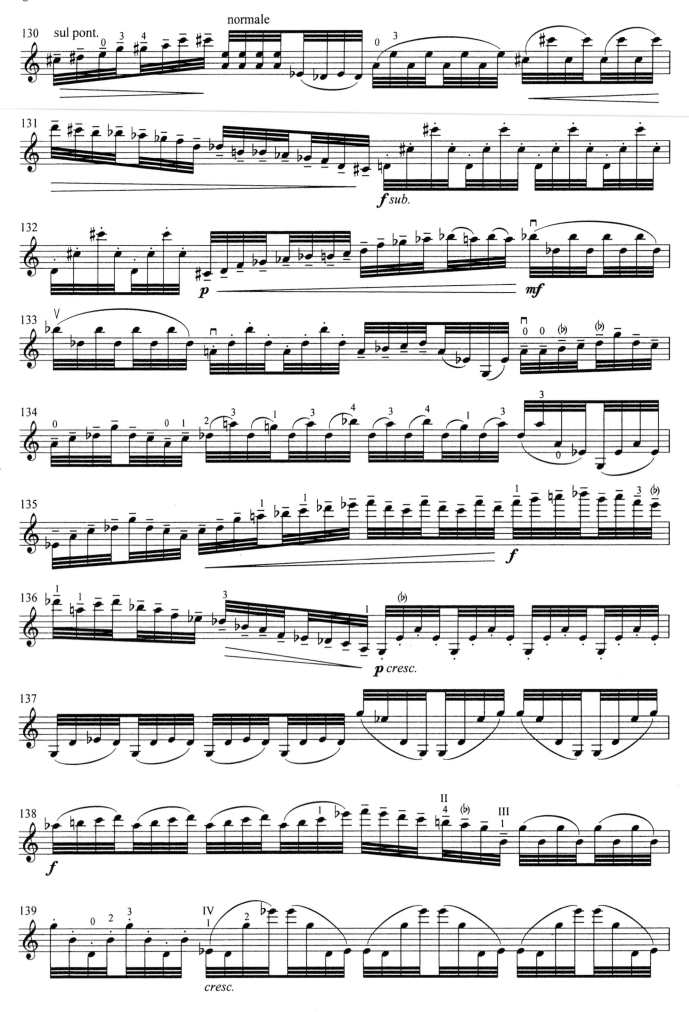

Sipoo, Finland, 11 July 2002